The Way of GRATITUDE

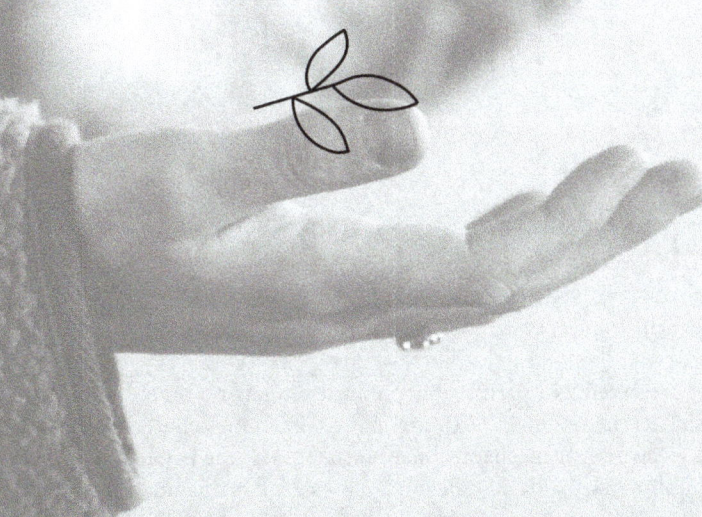

HANNAH ROWEN FRY

Cover and Interior Design by Nichole Lorinne Design. Title Photo by Jon Tyson on Unsplash.com. Author Photo by Ginny Stephens Photography.

All Scripture quotations are taken from THE HOLY BIBLE, NEW INTERNATIONAL VERSION®, NIV® © 1973, 1978, 1984, 2011 by Biblica, Inc. ® Used by permission. All rights reserved worldwide.

ISBN 979-8-9888954-1-1 (Paperback)
ISBN 979-8-9888954-0-4 (eBook)

CONTENTS

THE CASE FOR GRATITUDE

I first encountered gratitude as a way of life when I was in college and one of my mentors gifted me the book *Ruthless Trust* by Brennan Manning. Before reading this book, I always thought gratitude was synonymous with thankfulness. While the words can be used interchangeably, gratitude carries a much deeper meaning.

I was taught thankfulness as a child, and understood what giving thanks looked like. In other words, I had good manners and said "thank you" often, both to the people around me and to God. I remember my parents embodying gratitude mostly through generosity.

But in reading this book about trust, I began to understand the *way* of gratitude, that it is not just something we say or do, but that it is a way we live.

Gratitude is a lifestyle.

Gratitude as a way of life goes beyond politeness and manners. It oozes thanksgiving from our heart so strongly, we can feel it physically and emotionally. It's an expression of love, generosity, and humility. We can sit alone and be so deeply thankful we are brought to tears. We can dwell with others and strengthen our relationships by listening, an act of gratitude that says "Thank you for sharing your story - your vulnerability - with me." The way of gratitude is not just about keeping a list of what we're thankful for; it is an embodiment of the gift of salvation through Christ seeping into every part of our lives.

1

Throughout this journal, you will be asked to reflect, to question, and to wonder. There are two primary functions of wonder: *curiosity* and *awe*.

- In curiosity, we ask questions. "I wonder what this means for my life?" or "I wonder why this is worth mentioning?"

- In awe, we marvel at God's mercy, character, and magnitude. Here we say, "Behold the wonder of God!" or one of my favorite hymns, "When I survey the wondrous cross..."

Both functions of wonder connect our hearts to our minds, deepening our faith and inviting us to abide in Jesus.

I suggest reading these devotionals 4 days per week. This practice allows you to dwell and abide without the legalism of religiosity overtaking your time spent with God. Be aware that Satan wants nothing more than to make this time a burden. Perfectionist tendencies to read all 7 days per week have no ground here. Hold yourself accountable to consistent time with the Lord, but don't get trapped in the all-or-nothing thinking of studying his Word. Your salvation is not at risk if you miss a day of reading.

Finally, you may be asking what makes this book different? Gratitude journals are so easy to find, many of them free. Why should you read this one? Aren't there other books about living a grateful life? Yes, there are. But gratitude is one of the simplest and most challenging postures to unceasingly hold in life. We will never stop needing to refocus our minds toward gratitude. So when you're done with this one, go find another gratitude journal. Or start your own.

Devotional Tracker

Color in the leaves as you complete each devotional. Remember, the goal is not perfection, just spending time with God in gratitude regularly.

ONE

Jesus Feeds The 5,000

MATTHEW 14:13-21

✦✦✦

Write what leads you to wonder, in curiosity and in awe.

"Taking the five loaves and the two fish and looking up to heaven, he gave thanks and broke the loaves...They all ate and were satisfied, and the disciples picked up twelve basketfuls of broken pieces that were left over."

Matthew 14:19-20

Jesus Feeds The 5,000

Jesus fed thousands of people with gratitude. They ate this day because of his thankfulness toward God. Matthew tells us Jesus looked up to heaven when he gave thanks. Imagine the catalyst this posture of gratitude can be in your life, if it's what Jesus used to feed thousands! He could have called upon the angels of the Lord, the prophets of old, or the saints of heaven for a supernatural feeding. He could have commissioned all the bakers in town, the fishermen nearby, and collected an offering to purchase enough food for the crowd.

But he didn't. In his wisdom, he just gave *thanks*.

Gratitude leads to blessing. The crowds were blessed physically and spiritually in this moment.

Gratitude leads to sustenance. The people ate until they were full and fully satisfied.

Gratitude leads to miracle. Impossible things happen when we begin with a word of thanks.

Gratitude leads to abundance. They had more than enough food, plenty of leftovers! I wonder if anyone went in for a second helping?

Take a moment to write out what you are thankful for. It could be bread. It could be fish. It could be your family, your friends, your work, your mind, your favorite candle scent, your favorite coffee mug, your home, your faith, your vacation, and the list goes on and on! We're just getting in the practice of saying "Thank you, God."

It doesn't have to be significant or deep. After all, Jesus did a whole lot just by thanking God for a loaf of bread.

JOURNAL

_____

_____

_____

_____

_____

_____

_____

_____

_____

_____

_____

_____

_____

_____

_____

_____

_____

_____

_____

_____

_____

TWO

Jesus Feeds The 4,000

READ MATTHEW 15:29-38

✦✦✦

Write what leads you to wonder, in curiosity and in awe.

"Then he took the seven loaves and the fish, and when he had given thanks, he broke them... They all ate and were satisfied."

Matthew 15:36-37

Jesus Feeds The 4,000

Does this sound familiar?

Since we last saw Jesus feed thousands of people, he walked on water, healed a Canaanite woman's daughter, and put the Pharisees in their place (he does that a lot). He also explained to the religious leaders "the things that come out of a person's mouth come from the heart" in Matthew 15:18. Our heart-posture is expressed through our words and actions. If gratitude is in our heart, it is on our lips and in our hands.

Clearly, Jesus was a man of gratitude. His thankfulness flows yet again to produce a miracle of blessing, sustenance, and abundance to the crowds. I wonder if any of the same people were in this crowd, glad to be back for another helping? I wonder what gratitude-bread tastes like? Challah? Manna? Brioche? Focaccia?

Look back at your list from the previous devotional. Continue to write out what you are thankful for, either adding to it or getting more specific on what you've already written. As we have seen in the text, the miracle happens after we give thanks.

THREE

Pouting, Pity, Plants

READ JONAH 3:1-4:11

✦✦✦

Write what leads you to wonder, in curiosity and in awe.

"Then the Lord God provided a leafy plant and made it grow up over Jonah to give shade for his head to ease his discomfort, and Jonah was very happy about the plant."

Jonah 4:6

Jonah was a prophet who God called to go to Nineveh, a city of wickedness. He resisted, and was thrown into the sea by a group of sailors amid a violent storm. God sent a big fish to swallow Jonah to keep him safe in the water until he approached the shore. After three days and three nights, Jonah was released from the fish to go to Nineveh again, and he obeyed this time, proclaiming the message of God. The people of the city then turned from their wickedness and were spared from destruction.

I really admire Jonah in this passage for his dramatic honesty. Once he began to follow God, he led a whole city to be saved! But he got jealous and angry because he knew God's salvific character and did not want to risk his life to see it unfold. He knew God would be "gracious and compassionate... slow to anger and abounding in love" (Jonah 4:2), but he made Jonah do the work anyway. As a result, he went away to pout.

While he was throwing himself a pity party, God grew him a leafy plant. I picture Jonah, sitting on a rock overlooking the city, hot and tired, and a large plant grows next to him providing shade. The Scripture says he "was very happy about the plant" (Jonah 4:6). He switched from feeling enough anger that he wanted to die to happiness all because of a leaf! Such a simple act of creation put things back into perspective for Jonah.

What does this teach us about gratitude?
- Sometimes we need to step away from a difficult situation to gain perspective on it, i.e. to be grateful for it.
- Gratitude flows when we embrace the simplicities of life.
- Gratitude displaces anger. It is not possible to be angry and grateful at the same time. These attitudes cannot coexist.

List out some of the most simple things that exist in your life that you are thankful for. You may feel silly writing them. Embrace that feeling, and be grateful for the simplicity of it.

FOUR
Searching for Gratitude

READ PSALM 139

✦✦✦

Write what leads you to wonder, in curiosity and in awe.

"You have searched me, Lord, and you know me... I praise you because I am fearfully and wonderfully made; your works are wonderful, I know that full well."

Psalm 139:1, 14

Searching for Gratitude

God knows you.

You are wonderful.

These are two beautifully incomprehensible truths.

God knows everything about you, and wonders in awe at you. He knows your movements, your thoughts, and your words. His presence is always with you. Holy Spirit cannot leave you.

This is a great mystery to me, and a humbling one, that Creator God knows me intimately, even better than I know myself. He knows all the goodness in me, and he knows my jealousy, greed, self-indulgence, and dishonor. It's easy to think of our lives as scoreboards of what we do and don't do, but this is so far from the way God sees us. He doesn't just know us by what we do, he knows us by who we are, by who he created us to be. He defines us as his works of art, fearfully made with wonder and beauty.

The mystery, and perhaps the miracle, is that he continues to be in awe of us even in our dark moments, when we sin and when we are sinned against. The Psalm says, "even the darkness will not be dark to you" (Psalm 139:12). We were created by a God who consistently overcomes darkness. We serve a God who is not scared of darkness, because he created it, was surrounded by it once, too, and came through victorious.

Hearing how God sees me in this Psalm leads me to gratitude every time I read it. I am so thankful that he has given me life, eternal and abundant. Even in the moments of darkness I cause or experience, God still knows me and calls me wonderful. "Such knowledge is too wonderful for me, too lofty for me to attain" (Psalm 139:6). I am so grateful that God's thoughts are not limited to mine. His actions are not limited by me. He is so much greater than my brain can conceive.

Searching for Gratitude

Today, our gratitude journal is focused on God, on who he is.

Thank him for being Creator, for creating you, for being with you even now, for knowing you, and anything else that comes to mind that leads you to praise him.

As God has searched you, search your own mind and see what words of gratitude flow from it.

FIVE

Ask, Seek, Knock

READ MATTHEW 7:7-12

✦✦✦

Write what leads you to wonder, in curiosity and in awe.

"For everyone who asks receives; the one who seeks finds; and to the one who knocks, the door will be opened."

Matthew 7:8

Ask, Seek, Knock

Before we head much further into our practice of gratitude, it's important that we take a moment to ask Holy Spirit to guide us. When it comes to matters of the heart, there are two parties involved: us and God.

God has saved us by sending Jesus to live, die, resurrect, and ascend to cover our sins and restore right relationship with our Creator. God has given us life, physical breath in our lungs, consciousness in our minds, and abundant free will. We have access to him through Holy Spirit for the continued growth in our faith.

Our responsibility is to respond to God's invitation. We have a choice to make whether we will ask Holy Spirit to guide us into gratitude or not. Asking for opportunities to be grateful focuses our minds to see more of what we are thankful for, and what we focus on *grows*. For example, have you ever thought about buying a new car, picked one out, and then all of a sudden you see it driving around everywhere? Before you chose the car you wanted, it did not seem to exist on the road. After deciding, you see it on your street, next to you at the stoplight, and in the grocery store parking lot!

Jesus modeled a heart posture of gratitude out of which he submitted to the will of God, always. Asking Holy Spirit to produce a heart of gratitude in you while also choosing to practice gratitude will reorient your life. Pray for a grateful heart. It is a God-honoring prayer, and he will answer it.

Instead of writing today, change your posture and pray. Get on your knees, lay with your face to the ground, or stand with your arms or hands open to receive what God may have for you. Choose a prayer position that you don't normally assume, and in faith, boldly ask God for a gratitude-focused heart. There are words below to guide you, but feel free to speak truth and honesty from your heart as you cry out to the Lord.

Ask, Seek, Knock

Did you change your posture yet?

Holy Spirit, I surrender to your work in my life, to create in me a heart of gratitude. I pray that you would soften the hard parts of my heart so I may find something to be grateful for in every situation. I ask this of you, believing you can change my life as I choose to be thankful. I seek you, desiring to understand the heart of Jesus better and to follow your lead. I am grateful for your faithfulness. I trust you. Amen.

SIX

Working from the Overflow

READ COLOSSIANS 2:6-3:17

✦✦✦

Write what leads you to wonder, in curiosity and in awe.

"So then, just as you received Christ Jesus as Lord, continue to live your lives in him... overflowing with thankfulness... And whatever you do, whether in word or deed, do it all in the name of the Lord Jesus, giving thanks to God the Father through him."

Colossians 2:6-7, 3:17

Working from the Overflow

One of the benefits of salvation we often overlook is a life overflowing with thankfulness. We tend to think of the work of the cross as only an opportunity for eternal life. But in Scripture we see that abundant life begins when we choose to follow God! One of the ways we experience this abundance is through giving thanks to him.

This passage paints a clear picture of what overflowing with thankfulness looks like by suggesting what it is not. Lust hinders gratitude because it prevents you from loving your partner. Greed is the antithesis of gratitude as it puts focus only on what you don't have rather than the blessings before you. Idolatry leaves no room for gratitude when there is something you elevate above God, from whom all good things worthy of being grateful for come.

Our mouths cannot stand to speak anger or slander and "thank you" in the same sentence unless it is sarcasm. For example, "Thanks a lot!"

Following Jesus and allowing Holy Spirit to soften our hearts is a piece of salvation we can experience daily through practicing a posture of gratitude. It is a partnership we embark on when we say "yes" to Jesus. We have been given fullness in Christ, and we choose how to embrace that gift with the guidance of Holy Spirit.

Today, choose gratitude. Approach your work, your family, your body, your bank account, your home, and your community as you think someone overflowing with gratitude would. Pay attention to the moments when this is hard and journal about that. Don't try to do it perfectly. Just practice what you think it would look like and record your thoughts. Exercise your gratitude muscles as Holy Spirit grows and strengthens them.

SEVEN

Wheat & Weeds

Read Matthew 13:24-30

✦✦✦

Write what leads you to wonder, in curiosity and in awe.

"When the wheat sprouted and formed heads, then the weeds also appeared."

Matthew 13:26

This is the story of a man who planted wheat in his field and his enemy who snuck onto his property in the middle of the night to plant weeds there. The farmer and his family did not see the enemy coming; they did not hear him or notice him at all. In fact, the enemy must have done a good job covering his tracks, because the farmer didn't even notice the soil had been turned!

So the farmer tended to his field like he normally would, unaware of what else was there. He unknowingly watered, fertilized, nurtured, and tended to the weeds. I wonder if he spent extra money on labor tending to his field which was growing more than he planted? Did it cost him more money or more time away from his family to work in his polluted field?

Imagine how he felt after the wheat began to sprout. He was probably proud of his work, a return on his investment and a beautiful display of growth. But next to his bounty, he began to notice something else. It wasn't what he planted, not what he wanted, and not what he was working for. It was *bad*. It could not be sold. It could not be turned into food for his family. Plus, it was taking up space and valuable nutrients from the seeds he was tending to that could produce something more for him.

On top of that, his field-workers doubted him! They asked "Didn't you sow good seed in your field? Where then did the weeds come from?" (Matthew 13:27). Imagine the farmer's embarrassment, that he didn't even know what was growing in his field after all the time he spent working in it. He wasted valuable resources, and now his pride was hurt, too.

In this moment, he had a decision to make. He could pull up the weeds, ridding himself of embarrassment and lightening the load of his workers. Or, he could allow the weeds to continue growing with the wheat until it was time to harvest. Ultimately he decided to leave the weeds and continue to invest in them along with the wheat.

The text doesn't say he sought after his enemy to get revenge. It also doesn't say there was less crop because of the weeds. All we know is this unnamed farmer just continued on.

Gratitude is seeing and celebrating the good around you. As we practice gratitude, we become more aligned with the perspective of the farmer. Our lives, just like the field, are full of good and bad moments. There is no way to avoid weeds, no matter how much we care for our wheat. Living a life with a posture of gratitude shifts our focus toward the good, despite the weeds that threaten to shift our focus away from it.

What is the wheat in your life? What are the weeds in your life that distract you from the wheat? Get specific, and spend some time journaling these questions. Ask Holy Spirit to guide you as you write.

How is your life different when you're focused on wheat? How is your life different when you focus on the weeds? Is there anything holding you back from being like the farmer, and focusing on the wheat even while the weeds are still there? What would it look like to practice gratitude in your field, seeing and celebrating the good around you no matter what?

EIGHT

Jesus Prays for the Kids

READ MATTHEW 19:13-15

✦✦✦

Write what leads you to wonder, in curiosity and in awe.

"Then people brought little children to Jesus for him to place his hands on them and pray for them. But the disciples rebuked them. Jesus said, 'Let the little children come to me, and do not hinder them, for the kingdom of heaven belongs to such as these.' When he had placed his hands on them, he went on from there."

Matthew 19:13-15

Children offer us a unique glimpse into the kingdom of God. They are curious, open, unashamed, and loving. They exude joy, hope, comic relief, and often see the good in others. As adults, we get distracted so easily by money, chores, responsibilities, relationships, and survival in general that we may forget the simple beauties of life.

But we did not start that way. We started as children who were eager to do the right thing and saw the good in others. Gratitude was not something we had to exercise, not a skill to develop as we are practicing now. It is just the way of children. Think of the last time you gave something to a child that they wanted. It may have been a snack or meal, a toy, screen time, play time, or something else you know they desired. How did they react? Even if they didn't use the words "thank you," did you sense their gratitude in the exchange?

In this passage, children were brought to Jesus to be prayed for. It doesn't say if they were sick and needing healing or demon-possessed and needing freedom. It doesn't mention any calamity, chaos, or sin that they needed Jesus to save them from. It just says they came "for him to place his hands on them and pray for them."

Have you ever approached Jesus in this way? Do you know he prays for you, even now? Hebrews 7:24-25 reminds us, "but because Jesus lives forever, he has a permanent priesthood. Therefore he is able to save completely those who come to God through him, because he always lives to intercede for them."

We will never know Jesus without needing something from him, but we do not have to approach him only when we need something. This scripture invites us to come to him like these children without an expressed need - just to be with him, just to sit with him as he intercedes for us.

Jesus Prays for the Kids

The disciples tried to stop the kids from coming, but Jesus interrupted! Those amiss disciples getting in the way; much like the stuff of life that threatens to hinder our relationship with Jesus and distract us from a posture of gratitude toward him.

The challenge today is to sit with Jesus as a child. Write about how you showed thanks when you were young. Come to him in prayer today with that same attitude.

"For the kingdom of heaven belongs to such as these" (Matthew 19:14).

NINE

Bread is All You Need

READ MATTHEW 6

✦✦✦

Write what leads you to wonder, in curiosity and in awe.

"Give us today our daily bread."

Matthew 6:11

Bread is All You Need

Matthew 5-7 is one of the most commonly taught passages of scripture, known as the Sermon on the Mount. In it, Jesus shares the way to live a righteous life. He offers a heavenly perspective on the law, love, generosity, prayer, fasting, judgment, and so much more. Many of the things he shared in this teaching were alterations of what the people had heard before. He spoke of righteousness and the kingdom in much more simple terms than what they had previously learned, free from laws and doing the "right" thing. Instead, everything he shared had more to do with *heart* than with action.

In practicing righteousness, Jesus says to pray, "Give us today our daily bread." Wouldn't you think he would instruct us to pray bigger? To pray for more? To pray for everything we need?

What if asking for our daily bread is asking for everything we need?

Jesus says to ask God each day for just what we need for that day, and then says to not worry about tomorrow. The audacity! But why would we worry about tomorrow if we are going to ask just for what we need today? We'll ask tomorrow for what we need tomorrow. And the next day we'll ask for what we need that day. But for today, we're taught to ask for just our bread for today. We've already seen what Jesus can do with a little bread...

Say this prayer to God today, showing gratitude to the one who provides.

God in heaven, your name is holy. I pray for your will to be done in my life. Give me exactly what I need for today. Forgive me as I forgive others. Keep me from being tempted to put my trust in anyone or anything but you. I know I am valuable to you, and you will provide me with all that I need. I am grateful you have told me to not worry about tomorrow. Thank you for the opportunity to focus on you today. Remove the burden of my future from my care. Help me to remember what a gift it is that you are already taking care of it. Amen.

TEN

Know More Than You Understand

READ PHILIPPIANS 4:4-9

✦✦✦

Write what leads you to wonder, in curiosity and in awe.

"With thanksgiving, present your requests to God. And the peace of God, which transcends all understanding, will guard your hearts and your minds in Christ Jesus."

Philippians 4:6-7

I like to learn. I like to know things. If you ask my husband, information is my love language. I was and still am a really good student. In school, it was common for me to finish homework the day the teacher assigned it to us, and not the night before the due date. I even read encyclopedias and the dictionary as a kid for fun! Nerdy, I know.

And then when I fully understood what was being taught to me, I asked my teachers for extra credit so I could learn more! The highest grade I ever got on a report card was 112.5% in one of my science classes.

So imagine my discomfort when I encountered questions in life that I couldn't read a textbook to find the answers to. For example, when people around me died unexpectedly, when my friends twisted my words and misunderstood me, or when my boss rescinded my time off request after already agreeing to it. Even reading Scripture didn't offer answers to these questions.

But what Paul tells us in his letter to the church in Philippi is that thankfulness points us to peace. Gratitude guides us to peace that transcends our understanding. I will probably not receive all the answers that I want. The older I get and the more I experience in life, the less I understand about it. Life on this side of heaven just does not make sense most of the time!

But Jesus did not come to answer all our questions, he came to give us abundant life.

Maybe abundance is found in the not knowing? Maybe ignorance really is bliss?

Know More Than You Understand

I am still learning to be grateful for what I do not know and for what I do not understand, trusting that it is not part of my daily bread. As we pray with gratitude, we can trust that God's peace is guarding our hearts from what we do not know.

Spend some time journaling with thanksgiving today. What are you glad you don't know? What are you glad you don't understand?

How can you trust God even when you don't understand how he is working in your life? How is his peace guarding your heart and your mind by not receiving all the answers?

ELEVEN

Fish is All You Need

Read Matthew 17:24-27

✦✦✦

Write what leads you to wonder, in curiosity and in awe.

"Take the first fish you catch; open its mouth and you will find a four-drachma coin."

Matthew 17:27

Fish is All You Need

Relax, I'm not going to tell you to be grateful for taxes.

But if that's where you thought this was going, maybe Holy Spirit has something else to say to you? You can take that up with him.

Reading this passage brings to mind the prayer Jesus shared in Matthew 6, "Give us today our daily bread." It is another example of God providing exactly what we need just for that moment.

What is astonishing in this example is just how casual it was to Jesus. Under the authority given to him by being the Son of God, he did not need to pay the temple tax. He was exempt from paying, and he really didn't have any money. He didn't make any money! He never took up an offering. He wasn't on a payroll anywhere.

Yet he paid what he did not owe.

It was just money. It was just a fish. It was probably very easy for Jesus to make it happen, this little miracle seen only by Peter. God provided exactly enough. I can picture this conversation, and Jesus almost annoyingly rolling his eyes at Peter, like "Yeah, I don't need to pay the tax, but it's just easier for me to create something out of nothing than to try to explain why to these people." Obviously, these are my words, but it remains true that this miraculous provision was casual and *easy* for Jesus.

God is still just as faithful now as he was in this passage. He still provides exactly what we need when we need it. In your journal, pray again for today's daily bread. Go back to the Matthew 6 passage for a guide, or write out a prayer in your own words. Thank him for his faithfulness, and for paying what he did not owe.

TWELVE

When Ingratitude Wins

Read Genesis 2:15-3:13

✦✦✦

Write what leads you to wonder, in curiosity and in awe.

"Have you eaten from the tree that I commanded you not to eat from?"

Genesis 3:11

Ingratitude was perhaps one of the first recorded human experiences in scripture; an experience that led to the fall. It was in the garden that Eve expressed ingratitude by acting as if she knew more than God. She was tempted to put her own desires and knowledge above the abundance her Creator had already given her.

She was in a beautiful, bountiful garden with everything imaginable at her fingertips. Picture the flowers and plants in perfect bloom, without mold or brown spots. Picture the rivers flowing a perfect stream of crystal clear water, the birds singing melodies better than any song.

How could Adam and Eve have been in that space and wanted *more*? The only thing placed above them in the world was God; they had dominion over everything else. Pursuing the one thing they were asked not to have instead of relishing what they were already given was the first sin. Ingratitude tells us that what we have is not enough.

Ingratitude exposes our shame. Adam and Eve didn't know they were naked until they ate.

Ingratitude is idolatry. It's one way we tell God we know what's better for us than he does.

Ingratitude prevents worship. Adam and Eve hid from God. It is not possible to worship and hide.

Blame was introduced to the world in this act of ingratitude, too. Adam blamed both Eve and God for his sin, saying "The woman you put here with me - she gave me some fruit from the tree" (Genesis 3:12).

When Ingratitude Wins

In a perfect world, we would walk with God in gratitude with no shame, no idolatry, no blame. Although the world we live in is not perfect, God is. Despite the imperfections, we can walk in gratitude with him.

Practicing gratitude is one way we fight against shame and idolatry.

Are you focused on what you don't have rather than reveling in the garden God has given you? Is there anything that has distracted you from worshiping him freely?

Journal about this today, noticing where shame tries to invite itself in. Write with curiosity, not judgement, showing yourself the same kind of grace God offered these first humans when his response to their sin was not condemnation, but a question rooted in belonging, "Where are you?" (Genesis 3:9).

THIRTEEN

Clothed in Gratitude

READ GENESIS 3:14-23

✦✦✦

Write what leads you to wonder, in curiosity and in awe.

"The Lord God made garments of skin for Adam and his wife and clothed them."

Genesis 3:21

Imagine living in a perfect world. The weather is perfect. The flowers smell good. You are walking freely with God, and have perfect love with your spouse. There is nothing bad here.

Then, in one moment, it is ruined. You make the wrong choice. And now it's raining and you don't have an umbrella, the flowers start to rot and stink, and you are instantly arguing with your partner. You feel embarrassment and overwhelming shame.

But God is still there walking.

Then when he sees your shame, knowing your mistake, he responds with a gift. He doesn't shy away from stating the new imperfect reality of the world you live in - our choices have consequences, after all. But he has *compassion*.

After the fall, God clothed Adam and Eve. The only recorded feeling we see in this passage is shame because of their nakedness, and God gifted them with garments, covering their shame. It is the first account in Scripture of him fixing our failures.

What is our natural response to receiving a gift? Gratitude.

Gratitude heals our shame. Accepting the garments with humility brought Adam and Eve back into relationship with each other and with God.

Gratitude replaces idolatry. In receiving the clothing, they understood their rightful place with God. He is the giver of good things.

Gratitude enables worship. By receiving what God has for us, we honor him.

The gift of God in this passage pales in comparison to his gift of salvation. If clothing can teach us this much about gratitude, how much more abounds in the cross of Jesus? God has been fixing our failures with his gifts since Genesis.

How do you respond when you receive a gift? In practicing the way of gratitude, we begin to see how everything we encounter is a gift: all of our days, the people we see, the jobs we work, and the good along with the difficult moments. What else in your life is a gift?

FOURTEEN

Healing is Serving is Healing

READ MATTHEW 8:14-15

✦✦✦

Write what leads you to wonder, in curiosity and in awe.

"She got up and began to wait on him."

Matthew 8:15

Healing is Serving is Healing

We often think gratitude is expressed by the words "thank you." While this is true, it is a limited understanding of both our words and our actions. Peter's mother-in-law shows us what actionable gratitude looks like.

Serving is the practice of gratefulness. Serving both softens our hearts toward gratitude, and it is a way to say "thank you" with more than just words. Gratitude in this text is a response to healing. Jesus touched her hand, she got up, and began to serve him.

Maybe she got him a cup of tea, a scone, and a blanket while he rested. Or more accurate to the culture, a glass of wine and some bread. I can picture the joy on Peter's face that she was better, although it was his mother-in-law, so maybe he would've been just as happy if she stayed in bed. I hope you can sense my sarcasm here.

The point is, a healed life serves. We are healed in serving, too.

This is especially true in relationships. It is very difficult to stay in an unresolved conflict while you are serving the person you are obstinate with.

Pick a relationship in your life that could use some healing, maybe a sibling, coworker, or in-law like in the passage. Write their name, and write a few ways you could serve them. This will be unique to each person in your life. It will not be complicated, but it does take courage to humble yourself to the point of *healing* through *serving*.

FIFTEEN

The Beginning of Nearness

READ MATTHEW 4:17-24

✦✦✦

Write what leads you to wonder, in curiosity and in awe.

"Jesus began to preach, 'Repent, for the kingdom of heaven has come near... Come, follow me.'"

Matthew 4:17, 19

The Beginning of Nearness

This passage marks the beginning of Jesus' public ministry. What we've seen so far in the New Testament before this passage is his miraculous birth and transcendent baptism. Now, upon hearing that John the Baptist is imprisoned, Jesus begins his work of preaching, teaching, and healing.

His ministry opens with two words: repent and follow. In practicing gratitude, I wonder if this is our start, too? Repentance heals relationships, first with God and then with others. And following Jesus is what it means to be a Christian, it is the first step in our relationship with him, the perfect example of gratitude.

Repent and draw near. Isn't nearness what we desire most in our walk with Christ?

I didn't understand what being grateful for the life of Jesus and the work of the cross was until I *drew near* to him. I had repented for my sins, turned from the ways of destruction in my life, but I didn't feel gratitude as I now understand it.

This comprehension came once I really committed to following him daily: putting him first in everything, before my career, before my relationships, and before my own self. My understanding changed when I submitted myself to Jesus as my *Lord* in the medieval use of the word.

This nearness drew a deep sense of gratitude from the depths of my soul, something I now feel so strongly I can feel it in my body even as I write this! Gratitude brings me to tears and literally warms my heart.

Today, the action is to surrender to Jesus. You will see your life and mood change by listing what you are thankful for daily, but a deep sense of gratitude that flows from you continuously and consistently only comes from following Jesus.

The Beginning of Nearness

If there is something you're still holding back, place God as Lord over it now. This could be a strained relationship, a secret, your worth, your career, control of your life or someone else's; the list of things we could focus on more than him is endless!

Lordship implies power, authority, and influence, three things that are safe in God's hands. The way of gratitude takes root in our lives when we repent and follow, when we submit, and when we abide.

Draw near to Jesus.

SIXTEEN

Worship is Gratitude is Worship

READ PSALM 100

✦✦✦

Write what leads you to wonder, in curiosity and in awe.

"Worship the Lord with gladness... Enter his gates with thanksgiving and his courts with praise; give thanks to him and praise his name."

Psalm 100:2, 4

Worship is Gratitude is Worship

Gratitude leads to worship.

Worship leads to gratitude.

The cycle continues.

And there is an abundance to be grateful for and worship! We are thankful for his love, for his mercy, for his compassion. We are thankful for the work of Jesus on the cross, for his birth, death, resurrection, ascension, and for the salvation that we receive because of it. We are thankful for Holy Spirit guiding us, working in us, pointing us to our Creator God.

These feelings of gratitude turn our hearts to worshiping the Lord. An abundance of gratitude flows from our hearts in the form of wonder and awe. We sit before him wide-eyed at his glory, marveling at the work of his hands, the nature of his character, and the magnitude of his heart for us. This worship then draws more gratitude out of us. It is a natural response to both praise him when we are feeling thankful, and to be thankful when we praise him.

In this passage, gladness and joyful songs are the expressions the Psalmist used to give thanks. Although worship is not limited to music, it is one way we participate in the act of worship.

Today, choose a worship song that leads you to awe, to wonder, and to marvel at God. Write out and reflect on the lyrics and the music. How do the words draw you to worship? How do the crescendos and melodies create space to worship as a sensory experience?

How might gratitude lead you to worship, and worship lead you to gratitude?

SEVENTEEN

The Last Supper

READ MATTHEW 26:17-30

✦✦✦

Write what leads you to wonder, in curiosity and in awe.

"Jesus took bread, and when he had given thanks, he broke it and gave it to his disciples... Then he took a cup, and when he had given thanks, he gave it to them..."

Matthew 26:26-27

More gratitude-bread. And gratitude-wine along with it! Amen!

This time when Jesus gave thanks for the meal, it didn't lead to a miracle of feeding thousands. Instead, it led to the forgiveness of too many to count.

Even knowing Judas would betray him, Jesus gave thanks for the meal and shared it with him. He gave thanks even though he knew one of his closest friends would betray him to the point of torture and death.

He knew what had to be done, and he gave thanks still.

Paul wrote about the way Jesus lived with gratitude and invites us to do the same: "give thanks in all circumstances; for this is God's will for you in Christ Jesus" (1 Thessalonians 5:18). Reading through the Last Supper and Jesus' final days before death helps us paint a clearer of picture of what Paul meant.

We do not need to be thankful for everything that happens to us.

We do not have to be thankful for the mistakes we make, the hurt we cause, or the pain that is inflicted upon us.

What we can be thankful for in every circumstance is the faithfulness of God.

Jesus was faithful in his earthly mission to live and die for our salvation. Holy Spirit was and still is faithful to come and be with us, continuing to guide us in Jesus' ways even now. God's faithfulness is part of his character, which cannot change. No matter what we do and no matter what is done to us, he *does not change*. This means that no matter our circumstances, we can give thanks to God for who he is.

The Last Supper

God's faithfulness allowed Jesus to have gratitude while eating with his betrayer. This mystery found in the Last Supper reminds us that God can be trusted. His faithfulness elicits our gratitude no matter the circumstance.

Spend some time reflecting on God's faithfulness in your life. Journal through these moments, taking note of the highs and the lows. Write about how these moments can be wrapped in gratitude because of his faithfulness, even if you're not thankful for the moments themselves. This may be easy or it may feel contradictory.

When Jesus gave thanks in this passage, forgiveness was the result. This forgiveness covers your sins, *and* the sins committed against you. For that, we can be grateful.

EIGHTEEN

Questioning Purpose

READ MATTHEW 11:1-6

✦✦✦

Write what leads you to wonder, in curiosity and in awe.

"When John, who was in prison, heard about the deeds of the Messiah, he sent his disciples to ask him, 'Are you the one who is to come, or should we expect someone else?'"

Matthew 11:2-3

Questioning Purpose

The role of John the Baptist in the gospels is a preparatory one. He was born not long before Jesus through a conception nearly as miraculous as Jesus' was! His parents were an unlikely couple: an older barren woman and a man who questioned God. He came preaching and teaching the people to repent as God's kingdom was coming near. His whole life's purpose was to prepare for Jesus.

And yet, when Jesus came, he wondered if it was really the Messiah he had been preparing for. John was more studied in the ways of the Messiah than anyone. His whole life, from even before his birth, led up to this moment. He was imprisoned, so he sent some of his followers to ask Jesus if he was who he said he was.

Most of the time when Jesus responded to the question of who he was (he was asked this often), he would turn the question back on the asker. But when his cousin and preparer John the Baptist asked, he gave a true, clear answer.

Jesus answered him in Matthew 11:4-5, "Go back and report to John what you hear and see: The blind receive sight, the lame walk, those who have leprosy are cleansed, the deaf hear, the dead are raised, and the good news is proclaimed to the poor." In other words, "Yes, I am the one you've been waiting for."

John came to preach repentance, encouraging the people to turn from wicked ways and keep their eyes set on God. His goal was to prepare the people's hearts to receive the love of God through Jesus in a way they had not yet experienced. Imagine the gratitude John felt when his disciples returned to him with this answer! Not only is he the one they prepared for, but he is *already* changing lives, showing his love through healing miracles and affirming John's ministry. Everything he had worked for became validated at this moment!

Questioning Purpose

We may want the confirmation that we're moving in the right direction - John the Baptist certainly did as he sat in a prison cell while trying to fulfill his life's purpose! But we do not always get to experience the fruit of our labor and see the result of what we've been working for. Kingdom living means we may not be the beneficiary. In the times we do see the outcome, we only see a snippet of it.

In these moments, practicing gratitude can motivate and encourage us beyond what we see. Being grateful to do the action ahead of us can be more fulfilling to our purpose than the outcome.

Ask yourself, "Would I still be grateful for [   ] if it didn't produce the result I desire?" and journal your answers. Fill in the blank with whatever Holy Spirit brings to mind: your purpose, a certain task, or anything else.

We don't often get to see the outcomes or experience the glory. But God does. Gratitude turns us back to him every time.

NINETEEN

Freedom in the Kingdom

READ MATTHEW 10:1-42

✦✦✦

Write what leads you to wonder, in curiosity and in awe.

"Heal the sick, raise the dead, cleanse those who have leprosy, drive out demons. Freely you have received; freely give."

Matthew 10:8

When Jesus called his disciples, he gave them a long list of instructions. He told them where to go, what to do, what to take with them, how to act, and to not be afraid. In the same speech, he explained the troubles they would face and the peace they would encounter.

What does this have to do with a lifestyle of gratitude?

Gratitude allows us to follow Jesus' instructions.

This is true of the disciples then and of us now. Upon realizing the gift of salvation we've received from him, that everything good comes from him, that he is faithful and merciful, that his grace abounds, and most importantly, that nothing we can do will ever separate us from his love, *only then* can we live out our callings.

The action follows the call. Our gratitude guides us to freely give what we have freely received.

With overflowing gratitude for the one they followed the disciples were able to produce fruit, heal, and cast out demons. They couldn't earn discipleship or create anything for the kingdom that God hadn't already ordained, but through gratitude they could participate in this kingdom work, giving freely to others what had been freely given to them.

Write about where you are in your life and how you can participate in the kingdom right where you are, guided by an abundance of gratitude. This includes your family, job, commitments, friendships, your body, social media presence, hobbies, and more.

The call of Christians is to not make these parts of our lives "spiritual" but to abide in God and share what we have received from him - the fruit of the Spirit - in these areas. How can you participate in this kingdom work today?

TWENTY

My Soul Longs to Praise

READ PSALM 103

✦✦✦

Write what leads you to wonder, in curiosity and in awe.

"Praise the Lord, my soul; all my inmost being,
praise his holy name."

Psalm 103:1

My Soul Longs To Praise

Psalm 103 captures the way of gratitude in a succinct manner. From the opening verse, "all my inmost being, praise his holy name" we can feel what the author David felt when he wrote. His adoration for God was deeply rooted while simultaneously overflowing. For the rest of the chapter, he explains why. He shares many truths about God that act as a catalyst for his overflowing gratitude:

- Verse 3 - forgives all our sins
- Verse 4 - redeems our lives from the pit
- Verse 5 - satisfies our desires with good things
- Verse 6 - works righteousness and justice for the oppressed
- Verse 7 - made himself known to us
- Verse 8 - is compassionate and gracious
- Verse 9 - will not harbor anger forever
- Verse 10 - treats us better than what we deserve
- Verse 11 - has great love for us
- Verse 12 - removed our transgressions from our identity

And on and on and on. His final explanation of gratitude in this Psalm is seen in verse 19, "The Lord has established his throne in heaven, and his kingdom rules over all."

The truth of God stated here deepens my gratitude for the Lord even as I write these words! He reigns above all, over the joys and the pain. You and I are always under his protection, always veiled in his love. What a shift in perspective! Upon realizing this, can we help be anything but grateful? David's response of praise in this Psalm invites us to honor God in the same way.

What does praise look like to you? It may include music, prayer, or Scripture. Praising God may occur in a specific time or place, or may happen in brief moments all throughout the day. No matter what it looks like or what it entails, praise is about communion with God. It's meeting with him, coming before his throne in awe of him.

My Soul Longs To Praise

As a subject of his kingdom, picture your heavenly father sitting enthroned above all, and meet him there. Praise him for his authority, his dominion, and all the benefits of being under his lordship.

Draw a picture in your gratitude journal if it's helpful, otherwise create it in your mind. Write out a prayer to this King of Kings, Lord of Lords. Meet with God here, with gratitude expressed as praise.

TWENTY-ONE

Alabaster Overflow

READ LUKE 7:36-50

✦✦✦

Write what leads you to wonder, in curiosity and in awe.

"As she stood behind him at his feet weeping, she began to wet his feet with her tears. Then she wiped them with her hair, kissed them and poured perfume on them."

Luke 7:38

Alabaster Overflow

I remember as a child in Sunday School we would yearly construct an alabaster offering box. It was a light blue cardboard box with pictures of tools on it. We would take it home and fill it with all the extra change from our houses - from under the couch cushions, the floor of the car, and whatever was in the laundry basket. The coins we were adding to this box were from the overflow. It wasn't a regular tithe, it came from the extra.

In the text, the unnamed, sinful woman went to a Pharisee's house for the sole purpose of meeting Jesus. Upon meeting him, she wept. Her tears were flowing over so much that his feet got wet with them. She dried her overflow with her hair, kissed his feet, and anointed him with the entire alabaster jar of expensive perfume.

The woman had no name in the text. She was only identified as a sinner. With much sin comes much debt. With much debt comes the need for much forgiveness.

Her response to much forgiveness was overflowing gratitude.

Jesus' final words to her are the full experience of an alabaster overflow, "Your faith has saved you; go in peace" (Luke 7:50).

Meeting Jesus changed her from a woman known as a sinner to forever being recognized as a woman overflowing with gratitude. Love poured out of her as the forgiveness poured in. As a result, she experienced peace, perhaps for the first time in her life.

Her faith led her to the Pharisee's house, her offering led to forgiveness, and her reality became peace.

The overflow of coins we would put in our blue boxes doesn't feel much like an offering compared to the faith of this woman. She entered the home of a judgmental religious leader, weeping, hoping for the forgiveness of sins and peace that passes understanding upon meeting a man she had only heard about but not yet seen face-to-face. Talk about risk! Couch cushion coins don't quite express this love, but total surrender to Jesus Christ does.

Write out a prayer of confession to God. Place yourself in the woman's shoes, allowing his forgiveness to flow in as gratitude flows out.

Just as she was unashamed of what it took for her to meet Jesus, identify and remove anything that may be in the way of kneeling at his feet with your alabaster offering. If it's helpful, assume the posture of kneeling, burying your face and hair into your floor as the woman did to the feet of Jesus.

May this exchange of confession and forgiveness be the catalyst for continued alabaster-overflow in your life, sharing peace and forgiveness with others as an expression of gratitude for what has been shared with you.

AUTHOR'S NOTE

When making a case for gratitude as a lifestyle, it's easy to assume that it means we ought to be thankful for everything and everyone. We can assume it means everything happens for a reason. Neither of these are true statements. Neither are found in scripture. Neither are aligned with the teachings of Jesus. If you journey through this devotional and come to the end of it thinking you ought to be thankful for the terrible parts of your life, then my goal has not been accomplished.

Christian thinking tends to sway to the extremes; black or white, right or wrong. In reality, theology and faith are full of gray areas. There are absolutes, which can be found in the Apostles' Creed:

🌿 I believe in God the Father almighty, maker of heaven and earth; And in Jesus Christ, his only Son, our Lord, who was conceived by the Holy Spirit, born of the Virgin Mary, suffered under Pontius Pilate, was crucified, dead, and buried; he descended into hell. On the third day he rose again; he ascended into heaven, and is seated at the right hand of God the Father almighty, from thence he shall come to judge the living and the dead. I believe in the Holy Spirit, the holy catholic Church, the communion of saints, the forgiveness of sins, the resurrection of the body and the life everlasting. Amen.

Beyond these truths which are essential to faith, much of what makes up our walk with Jesus is on neither end of the spectrum. It's in the middle, where there are more questions than answers.

The way of gratitude is a lifestyle which declares, "God is bigger than me and my life." It reminds us of his greatness in all things, while simultaneously recognizing our own value in the world. It elicits worship and humility while also exuding pride for our own growth, perseverance, and choices. It is a posture which always points us back to God, saying "I'm proud of who God made me."

It is being thankful for the breath in our lungs, the beating of our hearts, the thoughts in our minds, and the forgiveness of our sins. It is the inner knowing that in the end, everything is going to be okay.

It is inviting Holy Spirit to align our hearts with the goodness of God. It is the thought dwelling in the back of our minds that God can be trusted no matter what happens, and the action of choosing to trust him. It is not a feeling, it is a lifestyle focused on the one from whom all good things come.

It is the reminder that even though God doesn't cause our pain, he can heal it.

I pray you rest in this goodness, gratitude, and wonder all the days of your life. Amen.

Hannah Rowen Fry